Things to make for dads

Rebecca Gilpin

Designed and illustrated by
Samantha Meredith, Erica Harrison,
Non Figg, Stella Baggott, Katie Lovell
and Rachel Wells

Steps illustrated by Molly Sage
Photographs by Howard Allman

Contents

You could show your dad doing a hobby he enjoys.

Dangly dads

1. Draw the outline of your dad's head on a piece of paper. Using felt-tip pens, draw his hair and shade it in. Then, draw his face.

2. Carefully cut around the head, then lay it on a piece of bright paper. Draw a sweater or shirt below it and cut out the shape.

3. Lay the sweater on another piece of paper. Draw legs below it and cut them out. Cut shoes from another piece of paper.

You could press on stickers from the sticker pages, too.

For a chef, draw or glue lots of little squares on his legs.

Make your dad hold something by gluing his hand over the top of it.

4. Glue the legs onto the sweater, overlapping them a little. Then, cut out two hands and glue them onto the back of the arms.

Tape the ribbon on the back.

5. Tape your dad's body to one end of a piece of gift ribbon. Tape on his head, then attach his shoes with short pieces of ribbon.

6. Cut out paper shapes for pockets. Glue them on, then use a black pen to add details such as a belt, stitching and shoelaces.

Sporty dad T-shirt card

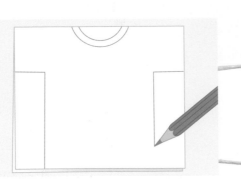

1. Fold a rectangle of thick white paper in half. With the fold at the top, draw the neck of a T-shirt, then add the arms and sides.

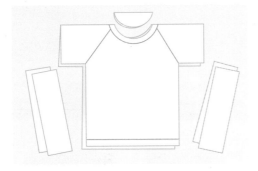

2. Add lines across the sleeves and the bottom of the T-shirt. Then, cut out the T-shirt, but don't cut along the fold at the top.

If you'd like to make a quick card for your dad, use one of the stickers from the sticker pages.

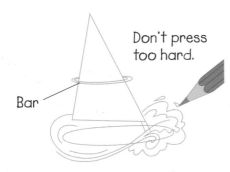

Don't press too hard.

Bar

3. Draw a surfboard, then add a mast and a sail with a bar. Draw curved lines over the board for waves, then add splashes, too.

4. Near the top of the sail, draw a small rectangle for your dad's head. Add his hair, an ear and his neck, then draw his face.

5. Draw a line across the bottom of the neck and add the shoulders. Then, draw your dad's body and arms touching the sail.

Even if your dad doesn't enjoy playing sports, you could draw his head on a sporty body.

Look at the cards shown here for ideas of other sports your dad might like to do.

6. Draw your dad's feet and the bottom of his legs on the surfboard. Then, erase the board where it overlaps the waves.

7. Draw stripes on the sail. Then, fill in the picture with runny paints. Paint the arms, neck and bottom of the T-shirt, too.

8. Leave the paint to dry completely, then draw over all the lines with felt-tip pens. Write a message to your dad inside the card.

To make a scene like this, add grass, flowers and bright butterflies.

Barbecue collage

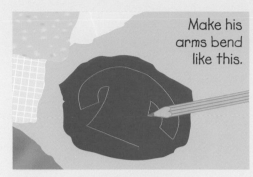

Make his arms bend like this.

Draw the apron inside the body shape.

Leave room for the barbecue below your dad.

1. Rip lots of pieces of plain and patterned paper from an old magazine. Draw your dad's body on one of the pieces, then cut it out.

2. Draw around the body on another piece of paper, then add an apron. Draw your dad's head and hands on another piece of paper.

3. Cut out the apron, head and hands. Glue the body and apron onto a large piece of paper. Then, add the head and hands, too.

Fill in alternate squares on the hat.

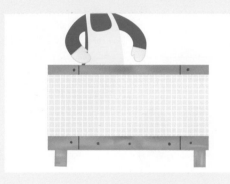

4. Cut out two tufts of hair and a chef's hat, then glue them on. Using a black pen, draw your dad's face, and add squares on his hat.

5. Cut a rectangle for the barbecue. Glue it over the bottom of your dad's body. Then, glue edges and two feet onto the barbecue.

6. Cut out and glue on lots of pictures of food. Cut out a fork and glue it onto your dad's hand. Then, add flames and hot steam, too.

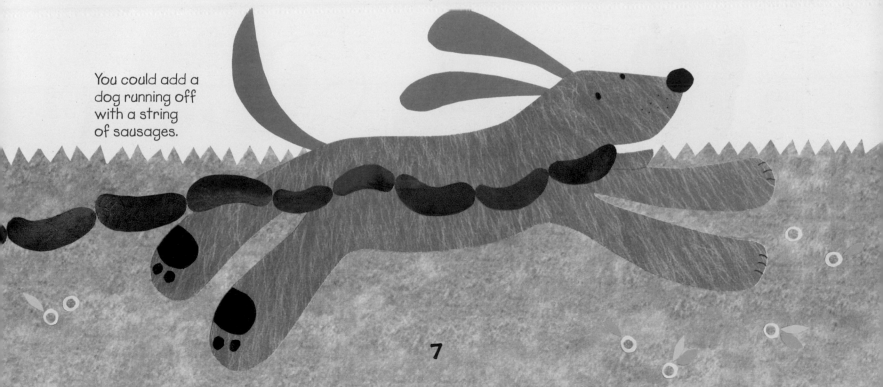

You could add a dog running off with a string of sausages.

Funky flowers

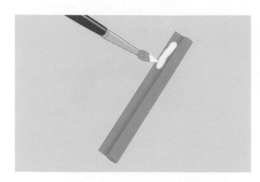

1. Cut a long strip of paper for the stem. Fold it over and over, like this, then glue the edge and hold it until it sticks.

2. Draw an egg shape for the back of the flower on a piece of thick paper. Make it roughly the size of an egg. Then, cut it out.

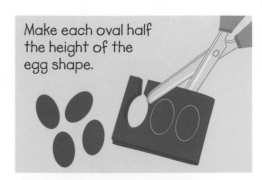

Make each oval half the height of the egg shape.

3. Fold another piece of paper in half twice. Draw three small ovals, then cut them out, holding the layers of paper together.

You don't need the other two ovals.

4. Fold ten of the ovals in half along their length, then open them out. Spread white glue at one end of each one, like this.

5. Press four ovals onto the egg shape, overlapping the top. Then, add three more ovals, overlapping the first four.

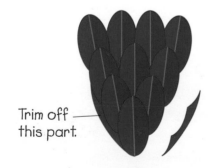

Trim off this part.

6. Press on two more ovals, then add the last one at the bottom. Let the glue dry, then trim off any of the egg shape that is showing.

Some of these flowers were made with textured papers (see page 15).

You could add more leaves on the stem.

8

To make a flower like this yellow one, cut out pointed shapes instead of ovals in step 3.

Add caterpillars and butterflies made from folded paper.

Make the ends of the strips pointed.

7. Cut several long thin strips of paper. Wind each strip tightly around a pencil to make it curl, like this, then carefully slide it off.

8. Tape the curls to the back of the flower, making sure that you don't squash them. Then, tape on the stem, too.

Glue the leaves onto the front.

9. Cut two leaves from paper and fold them in half. Glue them onto the bottom of the flower, then leave the glue to dry.

Dad heads

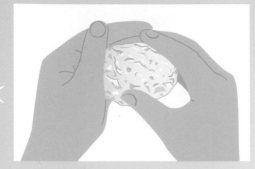

1. Cut a rectangle of kitchen foil. Then, scrunch it into a head shape, trying to make it look as much like your dad as possible.

Lay the head on plastic foodwrap.

2. Rip a piece of white tissue paper into lots of pieces. Then, brush white glue over part of the head, like this.

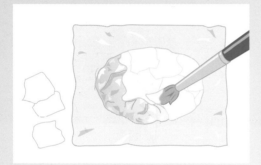

3. Press pieces of tissue paper onto the wet glue. Then, brush on more glue and press on more paper, until the head is covered.

4. For a nose, roll a piece of tissue paper in your fingers to make a sausage. Dip your fingers in glue, then roll the nose again.

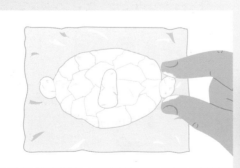

5. Press the nose onto the head. Then, roll two balls of tissue paper for the ears. Roll them with some glue, too, then press them on.

If your dad's going bald, don't glue on as much hair.

The beards on these two faces were ripped from tissue paper and glued on around the mouths.

You could make a grandad head, too.

You could draw glasses on a piece of paper and glue them on.

Overlap the pieces of hair.

6. For the skin, mix paint and white glue on an old plate. Carefully paint the head, including the nose and ears, then let it dry.

7. To make hair, rip lots of small pieces of tissue paper. Fold and pinch one end of each piece, then glue them all on. Let the glue dry.

8. Draw eyes on a piece of paper, then cut them out and glue them on. Draw a mouth, then paint pink cheeks and let them dry.

Pop-up goal card

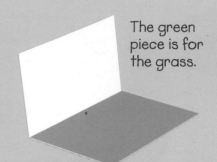

The green piece is for the grass.

1. For the card, cut two rectangles the same size from thick white paper. Fold them in half, with the short edges together.

2. Lay one folded rectangle on a piece of green paper. Draw around it and cut out the shape. Then, open out the card.

3. Glue the green rectangle onto the bottom half of the folded card. Then, fold the card again, with the green part on the inside.

If your dad supports a soccer team, you could draw him dressed like one of the players in the team.

Make sure that both cuts are the same length.

4. Make two small cuts in the middle of the fold, to make a flap. Crease the flap to the front, then fold it over to the back, too.

5. Open the card and push the flap through the middle of the fold, like this. Close the card and smooth it flat. Then, open it out again.

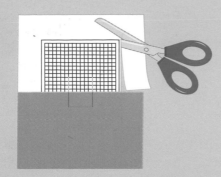

6. Use a black pen to draw a goal on the white part of the card, including the flap. Cut along the top of the grass and around the goal.

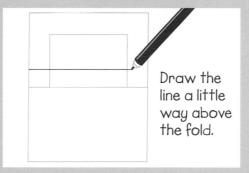

Draw the line a little way above the fold.

7. Lay the goal on the plain card and draw around it with a pencil. Lift it off, then use a black pen to draw a line across the card.

You could make a card showing your dad as a rock star instead.

If you put your card in an envelope, be careful not to squash your dad.

The fans need to overlap the goal a little.

8. Draw lots of happy fans around the goal, then fill them in with pens. Fill the gaps between them, and on either side of the goal.

Don't glue the flap.

9. Cut around the crowd, leaving a white edge. Glue the card with the goal onto the card with the crowd, lining up the folds.

10. On thick white paper, draw your dad saving a goal. Fill him in with pens, then cut him out and glue him onto the flap.

Bright coin box

These boxes were decorated in the same way, but with stars, spots and squares.

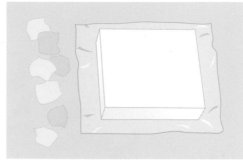

1. Rip lots of pieces from two similar shades of tissue paper. Then, lay the lid of a small box on a piece of plastic foodwrap.

2. Brush white glue on the lid and press on pieces of tissue paper. Continue until you have covered the top and sides of the lid.

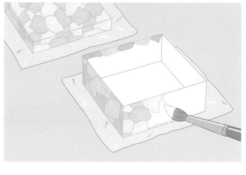

3. Brush the bottom part of the box with glue and cover the sides in the same way. Then, leave both parts of the box to dry.

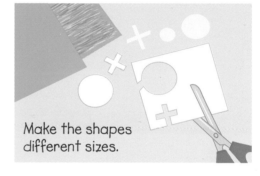

Make the shapes different sizes.

4. To decorate the box, cut lots of circles and crosses from thin cardboard, paper, tissue paper and textured papers (see opposite).

5. Glue a paper circle onto the box. Glue a smaller one on top, then add a cross on top of the circle. Rub the shapes to flatten them.

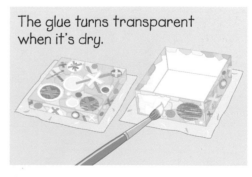

The glue turns transparent when it's dry.

6. Decorate the rest of the lid and bottom of the box with circles and crosses. Brush glue over the shapes, then leave the box to dry.

This is an ideal present for your dad if he leaves coins all over the place.

If your box has writing on it, add a second layer of tissue paper to cover the writing.

You could decorate your box with stickers from the sticker pages, too.

Textured papers

A brush with stiff bristles works best.

Scrunch the paper towel before you start.

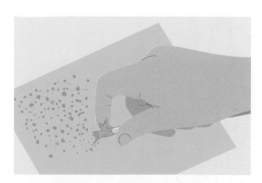

For brushed paper, dip a dry paintbrush into paint and brush it roughly over a piece of paper. Then, add another shade over the top.

To make speckled paper, pour some paint onto an old plate. Dip a paper towel into the paint and dab it onto a piece of paper.

To splatter paint over a piece of paper, dip a stiff dry brush into runny paint. Then, pull your fingernail over the bristles, like this.

Cityscape junk jar

The paper needs to be taller than the jar.

1. Cut a piece of paper that will wrap around a jar and overlap a little. Draw a line where the ends overlap, for a tab.

Don't draw on the tab at the end.

2. Unroll the paper. Draw lots of buildings on it with a thin pen. Add windows, doors and cars, then add details with a silver pen.

Your dad could put tools, pencils or other bits and pieces in a jar.

Hold the paper together while it sticks.

3. Cut along the tops of the buildings. Spread glue on the tab, then wrap the paper around the jar until the end overlaps the tab.

You could include famous buildings from around the world.

Tie card

Make the top edge straight.

1. Draw a shape for the knot of a tie near the top of a piece of thick paper. Then, add the long part of the tie below it.

You don't need to decorate the tab.

2. Draw a tab at the top of the tie. Then, draw over the pencil lines with a thin black pen. Draw lots of circles on the tie, too.

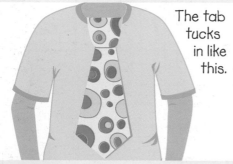

The tab tucks in like this.

3. Fill in the circles with bright pencils, then cut out the tie. Write a message to your dad on the back, then fold back the tab.

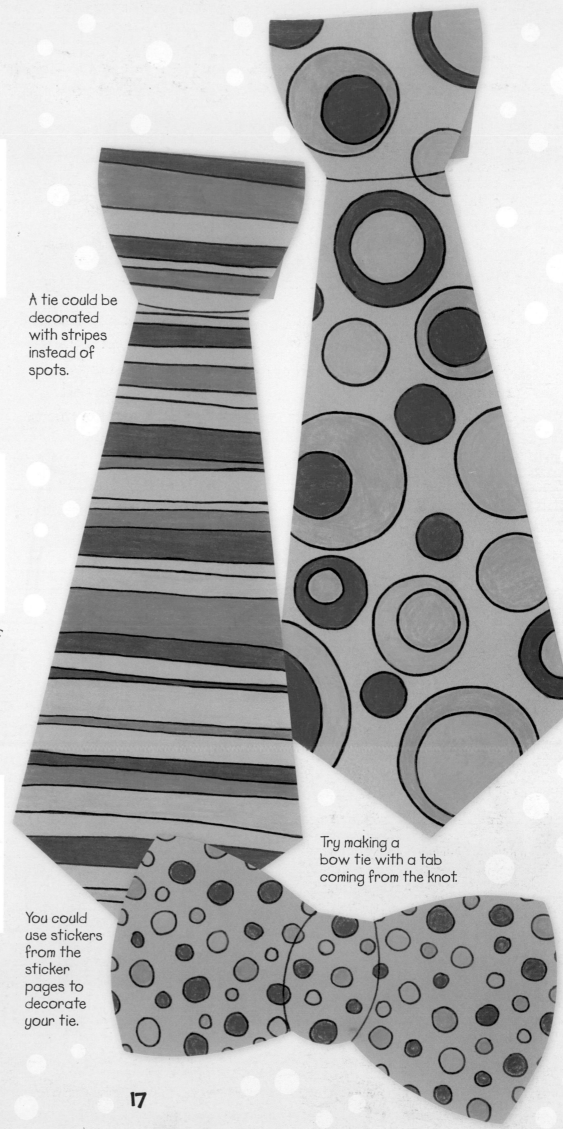

A tie could be decorated with stripes instead of spots.

Try making a bow tie with a tab coming from the knot.

You could use stickers from the sticker pages to decorate your tie.

Car photo frame

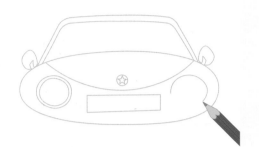

1. Draw the front of a car on a piece of thin white cardboard. Add details such as mirrors and lights, but don't draw the wheels.

2. Fill in the car with bright paints or felt-tip pens, then let the paint dry. Draw over the lines with a thin black pen, then cut out the car.

3. Cut out a photo of your dad that will fit in the car's window. Cut out a photo of you, too, then glue them both onto the window.

Look at this picture for ideas of different cars to draw.

You could make a frame to give to your uncle or your grandad, with their picture in the window.

UNCLE 1

TOP DAD

Tab

Glue the wheels to the back.

4. Cut two long, wide strips of thick black paper for the wheels. Using a pale pencil, draw zigzags on them for the tread.

5. Fold over one end of each strip to make a tab. Then, make two more folds in the strip, to make three sections, like this.

6. Press a piece of tape onto each tab. Press the tab onto the other end of the strip. Then, glue the wheels onto the car.

Try drawing a big truck instead of a car.

These cars have different patterns of treads drawn on their wheels.

No. 1 Dad

I LOVE YOU DAD

Sleepy dad door sign

Do not disturb...

1. Lay a roll of sticky tape near the top of a piece of thick white paper. Then, draw around the tape with a pencil.

Use the lid of a spice jar, if you have one.

2. Draw two lines from the circle to the bottom of the paper. Lay the lid of a small jar in the middle of the circle and draw around it.

Make the clouds overlap the edge.

3. Draw two curving lines, shown here in red. Add three cloud shapes on the curved top part. Then, cut out the door sign.

Erase the lines inside the hands, too.

4. Erase the lines inside the clouds. Then, draw two wavy lines across the sign for a sheet. Add your dad's head, hands and a pillow.

5. Draw three things your dad might dream about in the clouds. Then, add another little cloud below them, like this.

6. Fill in the picture with felt-tip pens and go over the lines with a thin black pen. Then, write 'Do not disturb…' on the sheet.

Do NOT disturb!

You could draw your dad working hard instead!

Flying lovebird

You could tape several birds onto a ribbon to make a chain.

Dad ♥
xx

Dad ♥

1. Draw a rounded shape for a bird's body on a small piece of cardboard. Add a beak and a tail, then carefully cut out the bird.

Lay the foil on the bird's body as you scrunch it.

2. Gently scrunch a piece of kitchen foil until it is roughly the same shape as the bird's body. Then, glue it on with white glue.

Lay the bird on a piece of plastic foodwrap.

3. Rip two shades of tissue paper into small pieces. Brush white glue onto part of the foil body, then press on a piece of tissue paper.

Wrap pieces of tissue paper over the edges.

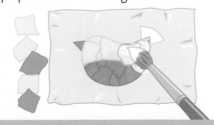

4. Brush on more glue and press on more pieces of tissue paper, until the bird is covered. Then, leave the glue to dry.

Use a blob of white glue.

5. For an envelope, cut a small rectangle from thin white cardboard. Glue it onto the back of the beak, then leave the glue to dry.

Dad

Dad
xxx

Try painting
stripes or spots
on your lovebird.

Happy ♥
Father's
Day

Daddy xxx

To my
Dad

For a simple
wing, just glue
on one tissue
paper shape.

To Dad

Happy ♥
birthday

A lovebird would make
a lovely gift for your
dad's birthday or
Father's Day.

Draw the
eye with a
black pen.

Dad

Only glue the
pointed ends.

6. Cut two pieces of gift
ribbon for the legs. Then,
draw two feet on yellow
paper. Cut them out, then
tape them onto the legs.

7. Tape the legs onto the
back of the bird. Then,
draw an eye on a piece of
paper. Cut out the eye and
glue it onto the bird.

8. Write a message on the
envelope. Then, cut three
feather shapes from tissue
paper for the wing. Glue
on the shapes, like this.

Nosy dad card

1. Cut two rectangles the same size, from thick white paper. Then, fold them both in half, with the short ends together.

2. For the nose, cut a short, curved line into the middle of the fold in one of the rectangles. Then, fold back the flap, like this.

3. Turn the card over, then fold the flap back on itself, creasing it well. Then, unfold the flap, so that the card lies flat again.

Try to make the hair look as much like your dad's as you can.

Happy Birthday

love Sam xxx

The flap becomes your dad's nose.

4. Open the card, then push the flap down through the middle fold, like this. Close the card and press the folds to flatten the nose.

5. Open the card. Draw your dad around the flap. Fill him in with felt-tip pens, then draw over the lines with a black pen.

6. Spread glue all over the back of the card, except for the nose. Press it onto the other folded rectangle, lining up the folds.

You can draw your dad wearing the clothes that he likes best.

You're great Dad   love George xx

Write a message around your dad or on the back of the card.

DIY dad painting

Use a pencil.

Draw this leg pointing down, like this.

Draw clothes that your dad might wear to do DIY.

1. Draw your dad's hair near the top of a piece of white paper. Draw the sides of his head, then add his ear, face and neck.

2. Draw two curved lines for the shoulders and the top of the arms. Add the bottom of the arms, then add his body and legs.

3. Add your dad's clothes and shoes, but don't draw his hands yet. Then, draw lots of splashes of paint on his clothes and shoes.

4. Draw one hand holding a paintbrush and the other holding a can of paint. Add splashes of paint and little lines to show movement.

Try drawing your dad doing other kinds of DIY, such as putting up shelves.

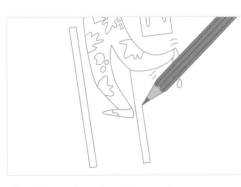

5. For the ladder, draw a long, thin rectangle to the left of the leg that points down. Then, add another one to the right of it.

You could also draw cans of paint, and a paint-splattered cat and its pawprints on the floor.

6. Draw two lines under your dad's foot for a rung on the ladder. Add lots of other rungs, then add the back of the ladder.

Make the edges uneven.

7. Draw a big shape around your dad for the paint on the wall. Draw shapes for parts that he has missed, and add drips.

8. Using runny paints, carefully fill in the picture, trying not to go over the lines. Then, leave the paint to dry completely.

9. Draw over the outlines of your dad with a black felt-tip pen. Then, draw over all the other lines with bright pens.

Dad's garden collage

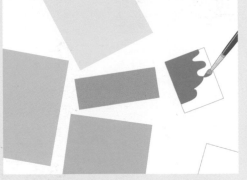

1. Brush lots of pieces of paper with different shades of paint for the trees, tree trunks, grass, soil and flowers.

2. When the paint is dry, roughly brush a darker shade of paint over each piece of painted paper. Let the paint dry completely.

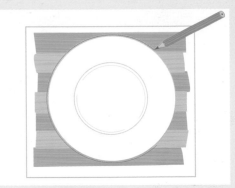

3. For the grass, cut several green strips and glue them onto a piece of paper. Lay a small plate on top and draw around it. Cut out the circle.

Make the shapes overlap the circle a little.

4. Draw around the plate on another piece of paper. Cut bushes and tree trunks from paper, then glue them around the edge.

5. Cut shapes for the tops of the trees. Glue them on, then glue the striped grass on top, so that it overlaps the bushes and tree trunks.

6. For flowers, cut lots of circles from painted papers and shiny papers. Glue the bigger ones on the bushes, with smaller ones on top.

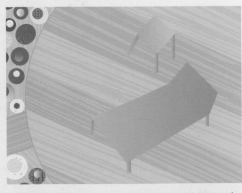

7. Draw a sun lounger and a table on a piece of blue paper. Cut them out, then glue them onto the grass, like this.

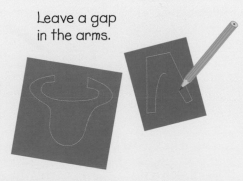

Leave a gap in the arms.

8. Draw a shape for your dad's body on red paper. Draw his legs on blue paper, then cut out the shapes and glue them on.

Glue the head over the gap in the arms.

9. Draw a face and hair on other pieces of paper, then cut them out. Cut shoes from dark paper, then glue on all the shapes.

Add other things, such as a shed or vegetables.

If you have a dog, you could add it sleeping on the grass.

29

3-D newspaper card

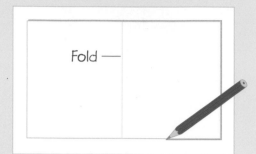

Fold ——

Draw the head in the middle.

1. Fold a rectangle of thin white cardboard in half for the card. Open it out, then draw around it on another piece of cardboard.

2. Lift the card off the cardboard. Then, using a pencil, draw your dad's head near the top of the rectangle you have drawn.

3. Draw a long strip for the arms across the rectangle, then add the shoulders. Draw shapes for fingers at each end of the rectangle.

You could draw your dad doing amazing things in the pictures.

Don't put the card in an envelope – it'll get squashed!

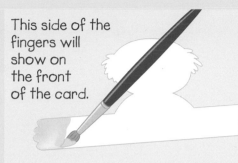

This side of the fingers will show on the front of the card.

4. Using runny paints, fill in your dad's face and add pink cheeks. Paint his hair, shoulders and arms, then let the paint dry.

5. Cut around the shape, then turn it over and paint the fingers. When it's dry, outline the fingers with a thin black pen.

6. Turn the shape over. Carefully draw along the edges and over the other lines with the black pen. Then, add a red mouth.

Write a message to your dad on the back of the card.

You could make a newspaper card for your uncle or grandad, too.

Trim off any pieces that overlap the edges.

7. Rip lots of pieces from a newspaper and glue them all over the card. Then, glue on paper shapes for headlines and pictures.

Glue the green side of the hands.

8. Write and draw on the paper shapes. Then, fold the fingers over and glue them onto the front edges of the card, like this.

I love dad picture

Start drawing near one end of the paper.

1. Using a black pencil, draw a circle for the dad's head on a piece of white paper. Then, add his face, ears and hair, too.

2. Draw a shirt and two stick arms, then add his legs and feet. Then, draw a girl's head a little way away from him.

Make the balloons heart-shaped.

3. Draw the girl's clothes, arms and legs. Then, draw a brother or sister holding her hand. Add balloons coming from their hands.

4. Fill in the drawing with pencils. Add lots of short green lines for grass, too. Then, write a message on each balloon.

You could add a bird in the sky and a flower on the ground.

You could draw everyone in your family as stick people.

I LOVE DAD

I LOVE YOU DAD

Christmas Fairy things to make and do

Christmas Activities

Halloween Activities

Fairy things to stitch and Sew

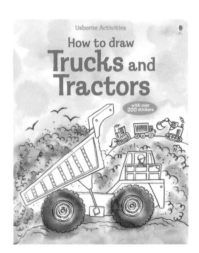

How to draw Trucks and Tractors

Christmas decorations and cards

Fairy things to make and do

Fairy Cooking

How to draw Princesses and Ballerinas

Valentine Things to make and do

Things to make for Mother's Day

Usborne Activities

Things to make for dads

This book is full of great things to make for your dad.
Whether it's his birthday, Father's Day, Christmas or any
other day, you'll find lots of exciting ideas for things to give him.
There are cards, photo frames, pictures, boxes and jars for
junk and lots more fun things, and they're all great
presents for grandads and uncles too.

There are also over 200 stickers
for you to stick onto the things you've made.

www.usborne.com

£4.99

JFMA JJASOND/09 091536

Not suitable for children under 36 months,
because of the size of the stickers.

CE

ISBN 978074606992-9

9 780746 069929

Perai, Malaysia